CORE SKILLS

PLAN IT:
CONDUCTING SHORT-TERM AND LONG-TERM RESEARCH

Miriam Coleman

PowerKiDS
press.

New York

Published in 2013 by The Rosen Publishing Group, Inc.
29 East 21st Street, New York, NY 10010

First Edition

Editor: Joanne Randolph
Book Design: Kate Laczynski

Photo Credits: Cover © iStockphoto.com/kate_sept2004; p. 4 Kamira/Shutterstock.com; p. 5 Ryan McVay, Lifesize/Thinkstock; p. 6 © iStockphoto.com/kali9; pp. 8, 16–17, 32 Comstock/Thinkstock; p. 9 Hemera/Thinkstock; p. 10 Jupiterimages/Brand X Pictures/Thinkstock; p. 11 Hulton Archive/Getty Images; p. 13 Dan Breckwoldt/Shutterstock.com; p. 14 Photo Inc./Photo Researchers/Getty Images; p. 18 Michelle D. Milliman/Shutterstock.com; p. 19 iofoto/Shutterstock.com; p. 20 Szasz-Fabian Ilka Erika/Shutterstock.com; p. 21 © iStockphoto.com/Tony Campbell; p. 22 Pixland/Thinkstock; p. 23 Digital Vision/Thinkstock; pp. 24–25 Caramelina/Shutterstock.com; p. 26 Michaela Stejskalova/Shutterstock.com; p. 27 Jupiterimages/Workbook Stock/Getty Images; p. 28 Toni Platt/Iconica/Getty Images; p. 29 Brand X Pictures/Thinkstock; p. 30 Comstock/Thinkstock.

Library of Congress Cataloging-in-Publication Data

Coleman, Miriam.
 Plan it : conducting short-term and long-term research / by Miriam Coleman. — 1st ed.
     p. cm. — (Core skills)
 Includes index.
 ISBN 978-1-4488-7450-7 (library binding) — ISBN 978-1-4488-7523-8 (pbk.) —
 ISBN 978-1-4488-7597-9 (6-pack)
 1. Report writing—Juvenile literature. 2. Research—Juvenile literature. I. Title.
 LB1047.3.C65 2013
 808.02—dc23
                    2012002141

Manufactured in the United States of America

CPSIA Compliance Information: Batch #SW12PK: For Further Information contact Rosen Publishing, New York, New York at 1-800-237-9932

Contents

WHY PLAN YOUR PROJECT?

Would you get on your bike and head to a friend's house without knowing where he lived and how to get there? Of course not. Just as it is important to plan out a trip, it is important to plan out a research project.

You can start planning by jotting down some ideas you might have about your project.

Sometimes your final project might be to present what you learn to the class. Planning for an oral report is different from planning for a written one.

A lot of work goes into putting projects together. When you are prepared, you will find it is easier to do a good job. Planning out your work helps you see how much you need to do and what resources you need to find in order to complete your project.

SETTING YOUR GOALS AND STARTING TO PLAN

What kind of project are you doing? Thinking about the type of project you will be doing will help you figure out the best approach to planning your work.

Will you be giving an **oral** report or writing a paper? Will you be building a **diorama** or making a poster? Different forms call for different ways of thinking and approaching the information you will be seeking.

Talk your topic ideas over with your teacher. Asking questions will help you define the project and come up with a strong main idea.

Once you know the type of project you will be doing, try brainstorming to come up with a topic that interests you. This means writing

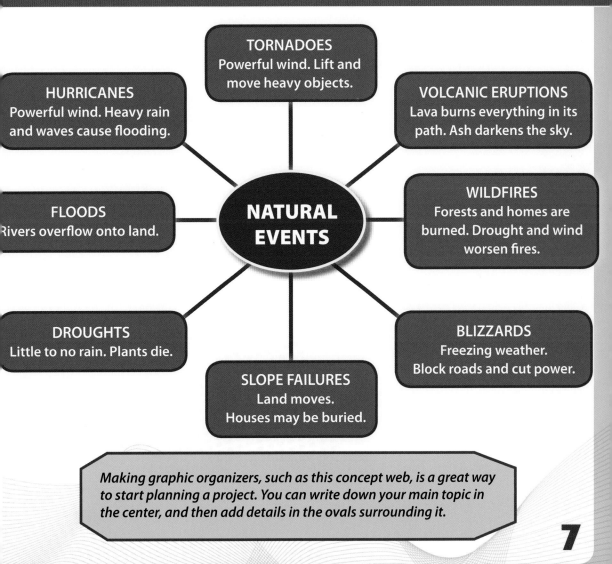

TORNADOES
Powerful wind. Lift and move heavy objects.

HURRICANES
Powerful wind. Heavy rain and waves cause flooding.

VOLCANIC ERUPTIONS
Lava burns everything in its path. Ash darkens the sky.

FLOODS
Rivers overflow onto land.

NATURAL EVENTS

WILDFIRES
Forests and homes are burned. Drought and wind worsen fires.

DROUGHTS
Little to no rain. Plants die.

SLOPE FAILURES
Land moves. Houses may be buried.

BLIZZARDS
Freezing weather. Block roads and cut power.

Making graphic organizers, such as this concept web, is a great way to start planning a project. You can write down your main topic in the center, and then add details in the ovals surrounding it.

down every idea that comes into your mind, even if the ideas do not seem like great ones. Your weaker ideas may lead you to better ideas. Perhaps you have been assigned to build a diorama showing an event from your state's history. Write down everything you can remember from your lessons

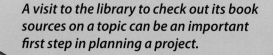

A visit to the library to check out its book sources on a topic can be an important first step in planning a project.

If you are doing a project like a diorama, part of your planning will need to include making a list of the supplies you will need to complete your project.

and reading, and write down your questions, too. How was the state founded? Who were the earliest settlers? Who built that tall skyscraper in the center of the capital? You can search for answers to these questions and think about which event would work best as a diorama.

QUICK TIP

Once you have a topic, do a pre-search to make sure there will be enough information to build your project around. A pre-search is a quick search to check that there are books and websites on the topic.

FIND YOUR SOURCES

Think about where you might find the information you need. Try to find at least three sources. The library is a good place to start. Looking in a library's card catalog or an **online database** can help you see what resources are available. You might find that many books have been written about

There are many great online databases that you can access through your school or local public library. Try America the Beautiful, BBC Animals, Encyclopedia Britannica Online for Kids, and the New Book of Popular Science.

Let's say your teacher asks you to research the Pilgrims. You could type "pilgrims" into Google and pick reliable sources from the result list. Sites that end in ".org" or ".edu" can be good places to start.

your topic. Sometimes, you might find that most of the information you need can be found in newspaper articles. You might even find film or **audio** recordings that are good sources of information.

You can also type keywords for your topic into Google or another **search engine**. This will bring up information from all over the **Internet**.

QUICK TIP

If you want to see quickly if a book has information you can use, search the index for keywords related to your topic.

PLAN YOUR TIME

Before beginning a project, it is important to understand how long it will take to complete it. This way, you can make sure you leave enough time to do the best job possible.

SEPTEMBER 2012						
Sunday	Monday	Tuesday	Wednesday	Thursday	Friday	Saturday
						1
2	3 *START RESEARCH*	4	5	6	7	8
9	10 *Begin Outline*	11	12	13	14	15
16	17 *Start Writing*	18	19	20	21	22
23	24	25	26	27	28	29
30						

Writing down the key steps to completing your project on a calendar will help you manage your time.

If you are doing a project on daily life in ancient Egypt, you will want to build in enough time to read a few books and websites on the topic. You might also want to plan extra time to visit a nearby museum with ancient Egyptian artifacts.

Let's say your teacher has asked you to research daily life in ancient Egypt. She then wants you to write a **fictional** story about a child growing up in ancient Egypt. Write a list of the steps you must take to complete the project. These steps should include researching the subject,

QUICK TIP

If you will be using books from a library, you should keep in mind that it might take time for the books you want to be available.

13

outlining what you have learned, writing the report, reflecting on what you have written, and **revising** your final product. Think about the time you will need for each step. Mark the date when each step needs to be completed on a calendar so you can easily see where you stand with the project and how much time you have.

Let's say your teacher wanted you to pick a key moment in the life of explorer Ferdinand Magellan to show in a diorama. What steps would you need to plan for?

CREATE AN OUTLINE

An outline is like a written map for how you will lay out the information you have learned. Outlines help you make connections between the different facts and ideas that you have gathered from

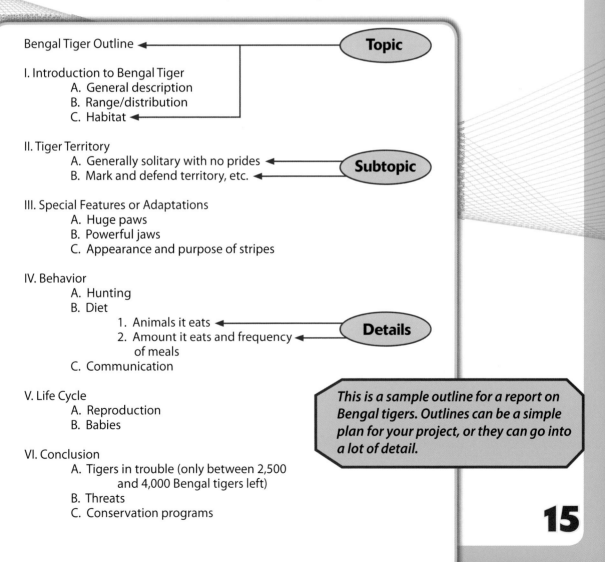

Bengal Tiger Outline ← **Topic**

I. Introduction to Bengal Tiger
    A. General description
    B. Range/distribution
    C. Habitat ←

II. Tiger Territory
    A. Generally solitary with no prides ← **Subtopic**
    B. Mark and defend territory, etc. ←

III. Special Features or Adaptations
    A. Huge paws
    B. Powerful jaws
    C. Appearance and purpose of stripes

IV. Behavior
    A. Hunting
    B. Diet
        1. Animals it eats ← **Details**
        2. Amount it eats and frequency ←
           of meals
    C. Communication

V. Life Cycle
    A. Reproduction
    B. Babies

VI. Conclusion
    A. Tigers in trouble (only between 2,500
        and 4,000 Bengal tigers left)
    B. Threats
    C. Conservation programs

This is a sample outline for a report on Bengal tigers. Outlines can be a simple plan for your project, or they can go into a lot of detail.

different sources. They help you see which parts belong together. They can also help you see when information you have found does not belong in the project.

The main ideas or topics for your project should be marked with a **Roman numeral**. After each main topic, list the details that support it. These are called subtopics. Mark the subtopics with a capital letter, making sure that you have at least two subtopics for every topic. You can even add lists of details to the subtopics. Mark these with **Arabic numerals**.

If you are writing a report about Mexico, you might choose geography, history, people, and culture as your main topics. Mark them with

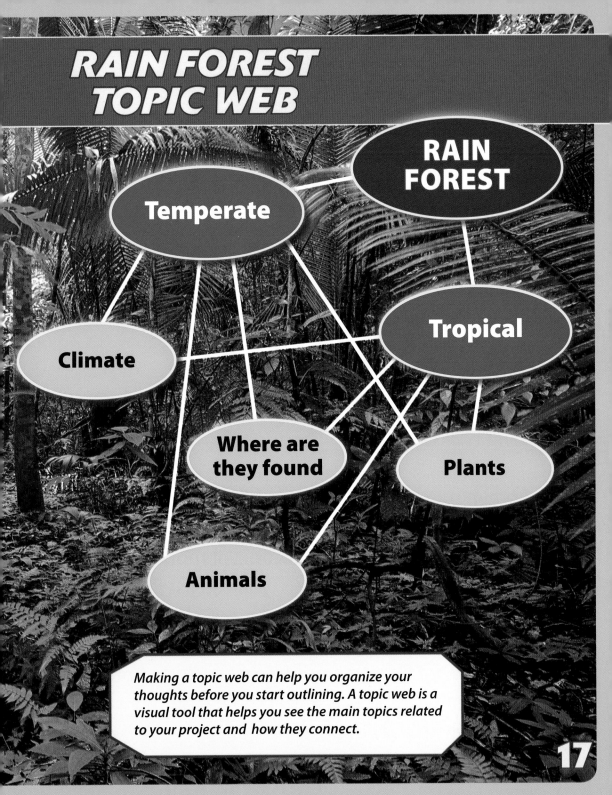

RAIN FOREST TOPIC WEB

RAIN FOREST

Temperate

Tropical

Climate

Where are they found

Plants

Animals

Making a topic web can help you organize your thoughts before you start outlining. A topic web is a visual tool that helps you see the main topics related to your project and how they connect.

17

Even if your project is to present your plan for a summer dog-walking business you could start, outlining will help. Topics for this project might include the supplies you would need and costs related to it.

Roman numerals. The subtopics under geography, marked by capital letters, could be mountains, lakes, and borders. Under the subtopic of mountains, marked by Arabic numerals, you can list El Pico de Orizaba and Sierra Negra.

As you learn more about your subject, you may find new details you would like to include. You can add your new findings under the heading or subtopic under which they fit best.

WHAT IS A SHORT-TERM PROJECT?

A short-term project can be researched and completed within a week or even just a day. You might do all the work in one sitting, or you might divide the work over several days.

If your teacher reads you a story and then asks you to write a plot summary or to come up with five questions you would ask the main character, this is a short-term project.

A short-term science project might require testing an idea, making observations, and drawing conclusions all in one day. A short-term history project might require researching a person's life using several different books and articles and then writing a report.

Brainstorming is a good way to start a short-term group project. You can also work together to find good sources. Try to divide up some of the work, though.

Let's say your teacher wants you to research the state symbols, such as the state bird, for your state. What would you do first to get ready for this project?

Imagine that your teacher assigns a project asking you to show how a bill becomes a law. Over the course of a week, you will work with other students in a group to research the subject and then present what you find to the class. Plan your time carefully because every hour counts!

> *How would you plan out the work for a short-term project for which you had one week to find out about the human skeleton and present the project to the class?*

First think about your sources. You might start with a general book that tells you how government works. After reading a short article about how bills become laws, think about what questions you still have and what would be interesting to focus on. You might choose to study how a recent bill became a law. You can then search for news stories about that bill.

If you are presenting with a group, you will want to spend time practicing your own part as well as scheduling time to practice together.

Take careful notes as you find information. Then work together to organize what you learned into an outline. Divide up the work so that each member of the group is responsible for one main idea or topic. Think about the best way to share the information with the class. Be sure to leave time to practice presenting your project.

WHAT IS A LONG-TERM PROJECT?

A long-term project may take several weeks or even months to complete. Since you cannot do the work all at once, you must make time for research every day or every week. Be sure to leave plenty of time toward the end to think about what you have learned and to tie the information together.

For a long-term science project, you might need to gather and record data over a long period of time. Then at the end you might need to draw a conclusion based on what you

Right Now

Sunny

50°F (10°C)

Feels Like: 45°

Past 24 hrs:
Precip: 0 in (0 cm)
Snow: 0 in (0 cm)

Wind:
From WSW at 13 mph (21 km)
gusting to 17 mph (27 km/h)

Through 8 pm: Sunny with temperatures steady or falling near 44°F (7°C). Winds WSW 10 to 15 mph (16–24 km/h).

Next 36 Hours

Today	Tonight	Tomorrow

nny	Rain	Partly Cloudy
°F (10°C)	34°F (1°C)	52°F (11°C)
gh	Low	High
ance of Rain:	Chance of Precip: 90%	Chance of Rain: 10%
d: W at 15 mph (24 h)	Wind: WSW at 9 mph (14 km/h)	Wind: NW at 10 mph (16 km/h)
ny. High near F (10°C). Winds W at 10 to 20 (16–32 km/h).	Mainly clear. Low 34°F (1°C). Winds WSW at 5 to 10 mph (8–16 km/h).	Mainly sunny. High 52°F (11°C). Winds NW at 5 to 10 mph (8–16 km/h).

have observed. For instance, you might study the climate in your area by taking down measurements such as temperature and **precipitation** over the course of the year. It might be helpful to create graphs and charts to show the data you have collected.

For a long-term social-studies project, you could research another country and make a scrapbook to

For a long-term project on a country, you might choose to have a section on a famous city in the country. If you are doing Italy, you might choose Venice.

As part of a long-term research project, this girl must present a different aspect of the Amazon rain forest each week. Here she shares what she learned about hummingbirds.

Charts and graphs can be good ways to show how things change over time. For example, a bar or line graph could show the temperature over a month. A pie chart could show what percent of days in the year were sunny, rainy, or snowy.

show all that you have learned. You might devote one whole week to studying each of several aspects of the country, such as its history, language, or food. Prepare a meal from traditional recipes and take photos of the food you cooked. Write down a song or poem in the other country's language along with its English translation. Leave time toward the end to think about what you have learned about this new culture. How is it different from yours? What did you find that is similar?

This student researched volcanoes for a science-fair project. For this kind of project, she needed to plan the way she would present her facts. She also needed to plan time to make a volcano to display.

PUTTING IT ALL TOGETHER

Research projects can seem like hard work at first. There are so many places to look for information and so many facts to keep track of. Time can slip away until you are left trying to cram a whole week's work into just a few hours.

> *If you plan your time and the steps of your project well, you give yourself the best chance to do a great job. Are you ready to plan your next project?*

If you plan carefully, however, you can break the work down into easy steps. If you organize your work as you go along, you will also find it easier to tie your project together at the end. Planning carefully can help you create a research project of which you are truly proud.

Glossary

Arabic numerals (A-ruh-bik NOOM-rulz) Any of the numerals 0, 1, 2, 3, 4, 5, 6, 7, 8, and 9.

audio (AW-dee-oh) Sound, especially when recorded.

database (DAY-tuh-bays) A set of data, or facts, held within a computer or on a network.

diorama (dy-uh-RAH-muh) A small scene, seen through an opening.

fictional (FIK-shnul) Having to do with stories that tell about people and events that are not real.

Internet (IN-ter-net) An electronic network that connects computers around the world and provides facts and information.

online (awn-LYN) Connected to or on the Internet.

oral (OR-ul) Spoken.

precipitation (preh-sih-pih-TAY-shun) Rain, snow, sleet, or hail.

revising (rih-VYZ-ing) Making changes to or improvements in something.

Roman numeral (ROH-mun NOOM-rul) One of the letters used to show numbers in the numbering system used by the ancient Romans.

search engine (SERCH EN-jin) A computer program that searches the Internet for websites.

Index

Websites

Due to the changing nature of Internet links, PowerKids Press has developed an online list of websites related to the subject of this book. This site is updated regularly. Please use this link to access the list:
www.powerkidslinks.com/cs/plan/